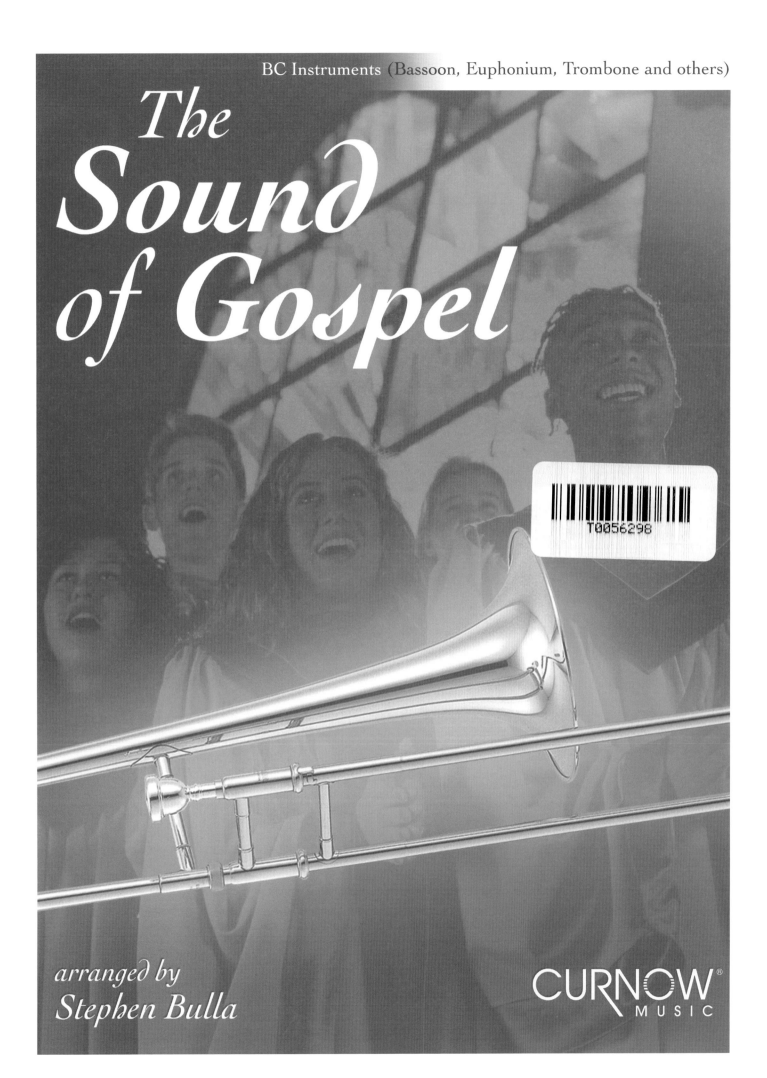

Order Number: CMP 1083-06-400

Arr. Stephen Bulla
The Sound of Gospel
B.C. Instruments

CD Accompaniment tracks produced by Stephen Bulla

CD number: 19-086-3 CMP
ISBN-10: 90-431-2427-3
ISBN-13: 978-90-431-2427-0

The Sound of Gospel

Introduction

This collection arranged for Solo Instrument (with CD track accompaniment) provides an opportunity to perform and practice enjoyable and familiar melodies in the Gospel style. This exciting genre includes a wide range of tempos and expressive lines written into the music, giving the soloist an enjoyable diversity of program material.

The book includes a selection of well-known Spirituals, well-loved Sacred songs, and up-tempo Southern style favorites. The solo parts always include a complete melody line and some variant of an obligato as well. A Piano Accompaniment book is also available. (Order number CMP 1084-06-401). These accompaniments are uncomplicated, yet fully portray the Gospel style grooves as often performed by well-known Gospel choirs and recording artists.

An accompaniment CD is included with the solo book for those times when an accompanist is not available. The accompaniment tracks provide the soloist with an excellent practice tool as well.

The Sound of Gospel

Arranger's Biography

STEPHEN BULLA received his degree in arranging and composition from Boston's Berklee College of Music, graduating Magna Cum Laude. He has entered his third decade as Chief Arranger to 'The President's Own' U.S. Marine Band and White House Orchestra and is responsible for the production of music that encompasses countless styles and instrumental combinations, most of which are performed for Presidential functions and visiting dignitaries in Washington DC.

His compositions are performed both in the concert hall and on broadcast media. According to a recent ASCAP survey his music was used in the last year on the following television programs: CSI Miami, Cold Case, Jag, Joan of Arcadia, Without A Trace, Guiding Light, Ren and Stimpy, 48 Hours, 60 Minutes, and Survivor.

Working directly with film score legend John Williams, he has transcribed music from 'Star Wars' and 'Catch Me If You Can' for performances by the Marine Band with the composer conducting. His musical arrangements have also been featured on the PBS television series 'In Performance At The White House' and performed by many artists including Sarah Vaughan, The Manhattan Transfer, Mel Torme, Doc Severinsen, Nell Carter, and Larry Gatlin.

In 1990 he was awarded the prestigious ADDY Award for best original music/TV spot, and later provided a music score for the 'Century of Flight' series on the Discovery Channel. In 1998 he was honored by The Salvation Army in New York for his extensive contribution to their catalog of published music for bands. That event included a 'Profile' concert of his compositions, featuring performances by the New York Staff Band.

His commissioned concert works include instrumental compositions that are performed and recorded internationally. The Dutch, British, Swiss and New Zealand Brass Band Championship organizations have all commissioned test pieces from his pen. His wind band compositions are published by DeHaske Music and Curnow Music Press.

Recent activities include a commission from the Library of Congress to complete and orchestrate the last known manuscript march of John Philip Sousa. That music with a recording is now available free from the Library's web site... (http://memory.loc.gov/cocoon/patriotism/loc.natlib.ihas.200000027/).

Stephen Bulla is a member of ASCAP (American Society of Composers, Authors, and Publishers) and has received that organization's Performance Award annually since 1984. He travels frequently as a guest conductor of 'All State' bands around the country.

Table of Contents

Track   **Page**

`1`   *Tuning Note A*

`2`   *Tuning Note B♭*

`3` `4`   *Amazing Grace* *6*

`5` `6`   *Down by the Riverside* *8*

`7` `8`   *Higher Ground* *10*

`9` `10`   *Rock of Ages* *12*

`11` `12` *Kum Ba Ya* *14*

`13` `14` *When We All Get to Heaven* *16*

`15` `16` *This Train* *18*

`17` `18` *'Tis so Sweet* *20*

`19` `20` *Sweet Hour of Prayer* *22*

`21` `22` *In the Sweet By-and-By* *24*

    Solo with accompaniment

■   *Accompaniment only*

Amazing Grace

Arr. Stephen Bulla

Amazing Grace

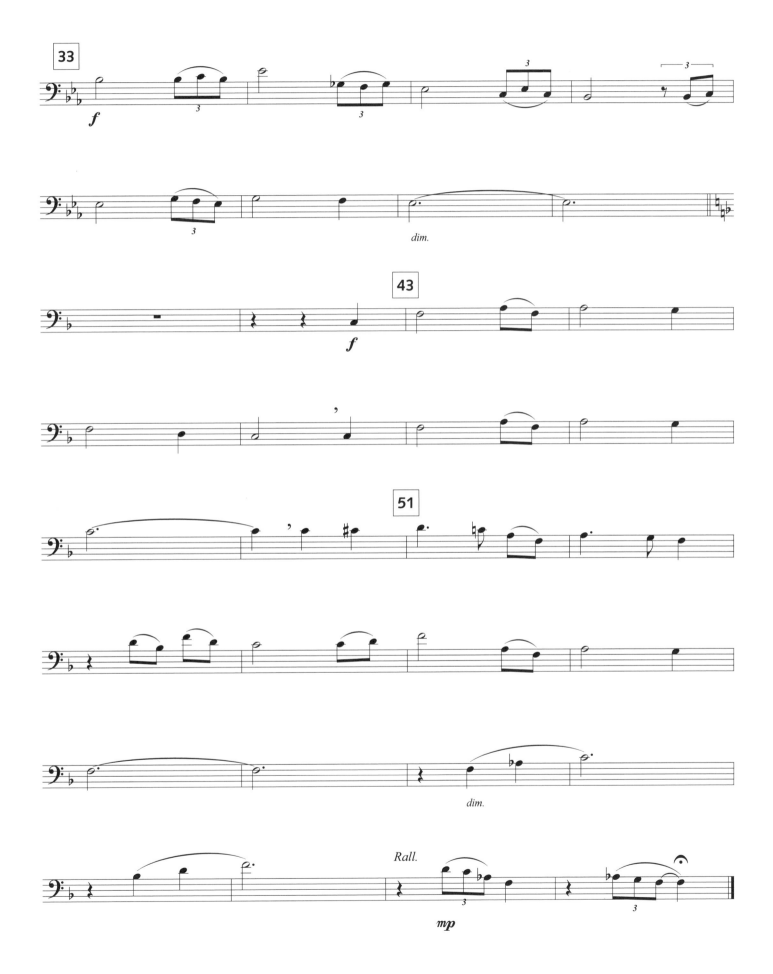

Down by the Riverside

Arr. Stephen Bulla

Down by the Riverside

Higher Ground

Arr. Stephen Bulla

Higher Ground

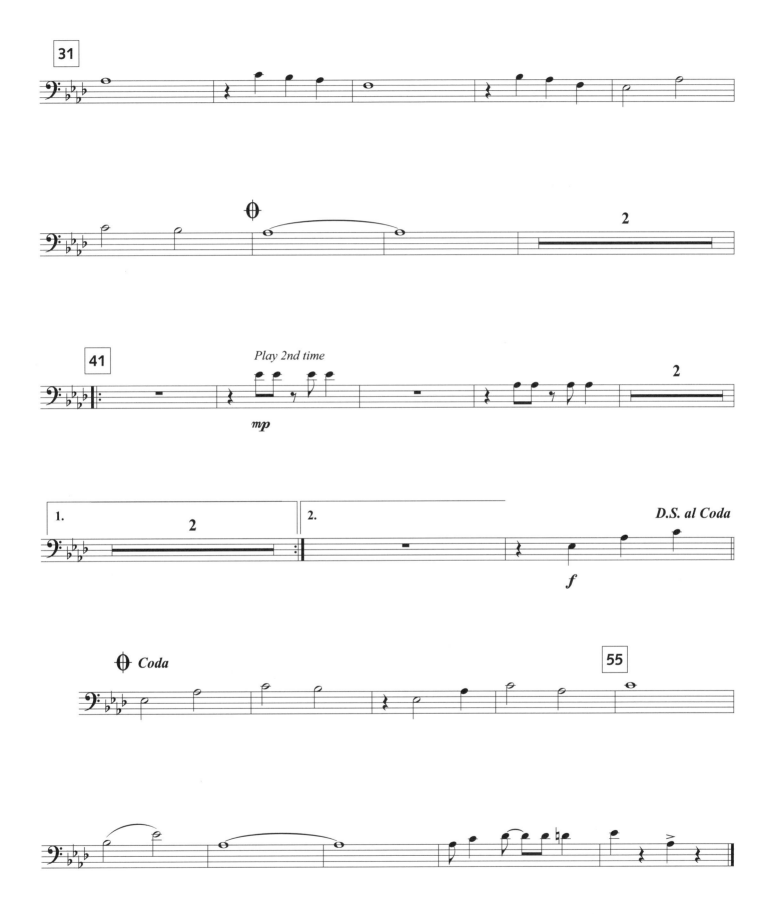

Rock of Ages

Arr. Stephen Bulla

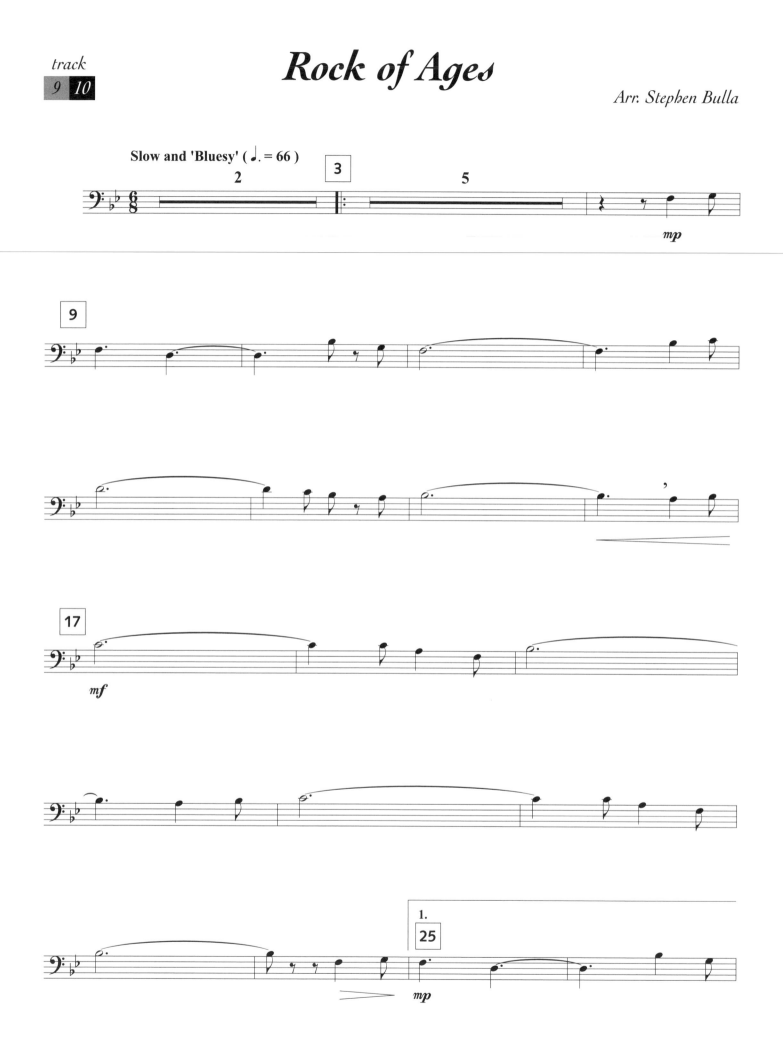

Rock of Ages

Kum Ba Ya

Arr. Stephen Bulla

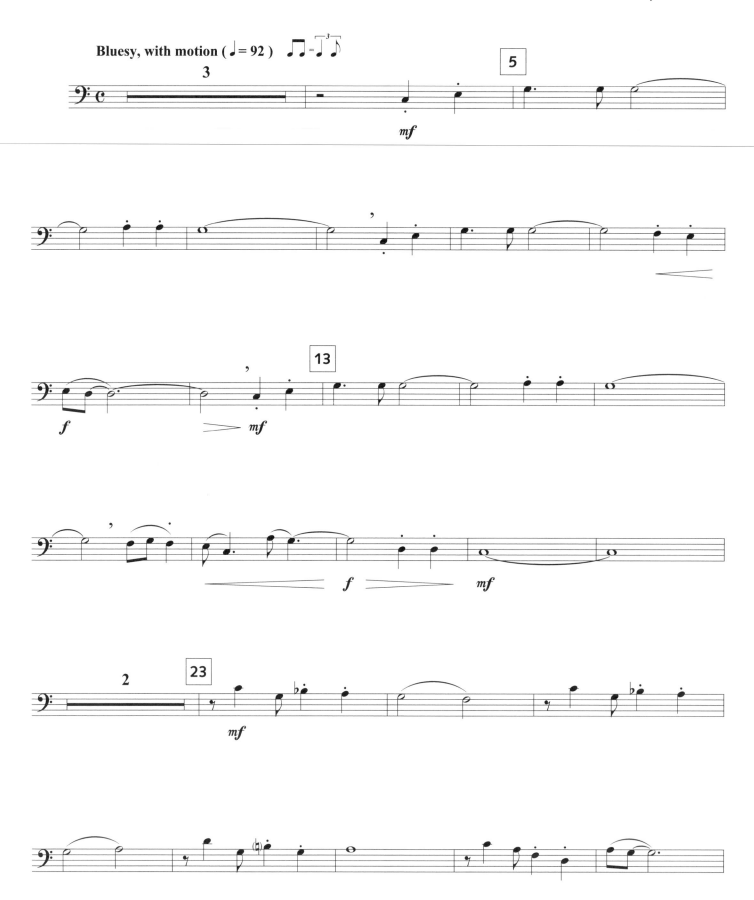

© Copyright 2006 by **Curnow Music Press, Inc.**

Kum Ba Ya

When We All Get to Heaven

Arr. Stephen Bulla

When We All Get to Heaven

This Train

Arr. Stephen Bulla

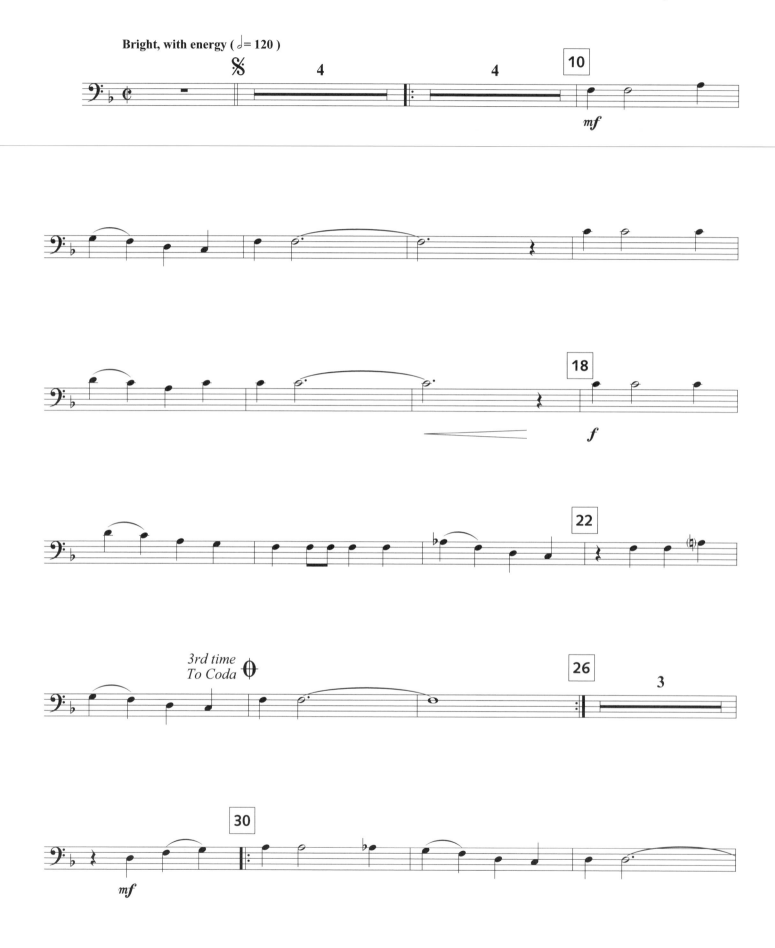

This Train

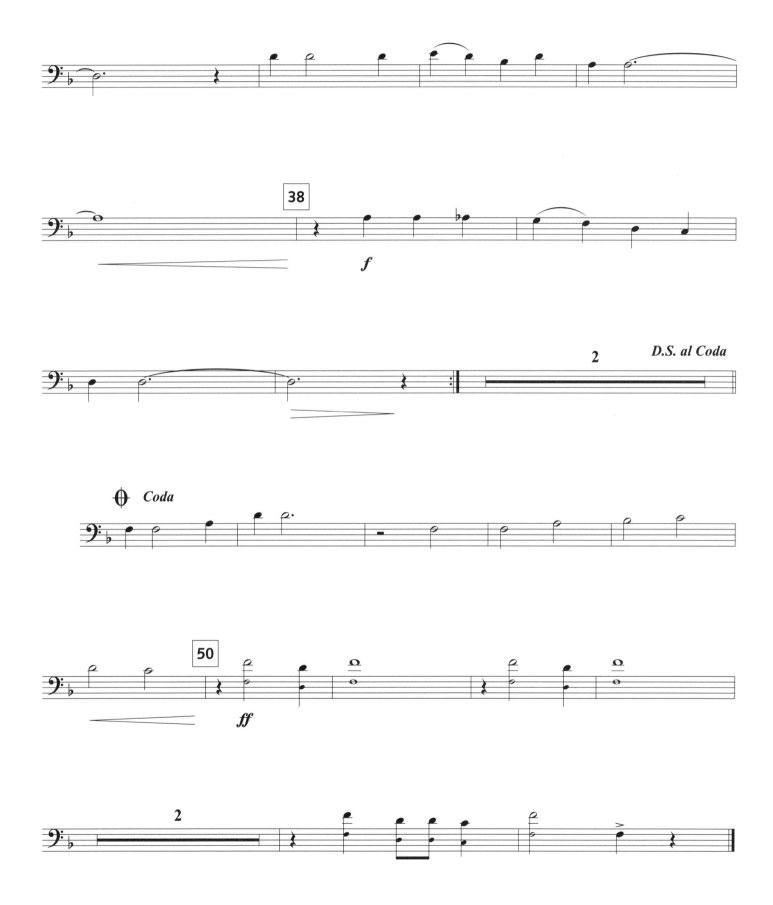

'Tis so Sweet

Arr. Stephen Bulla

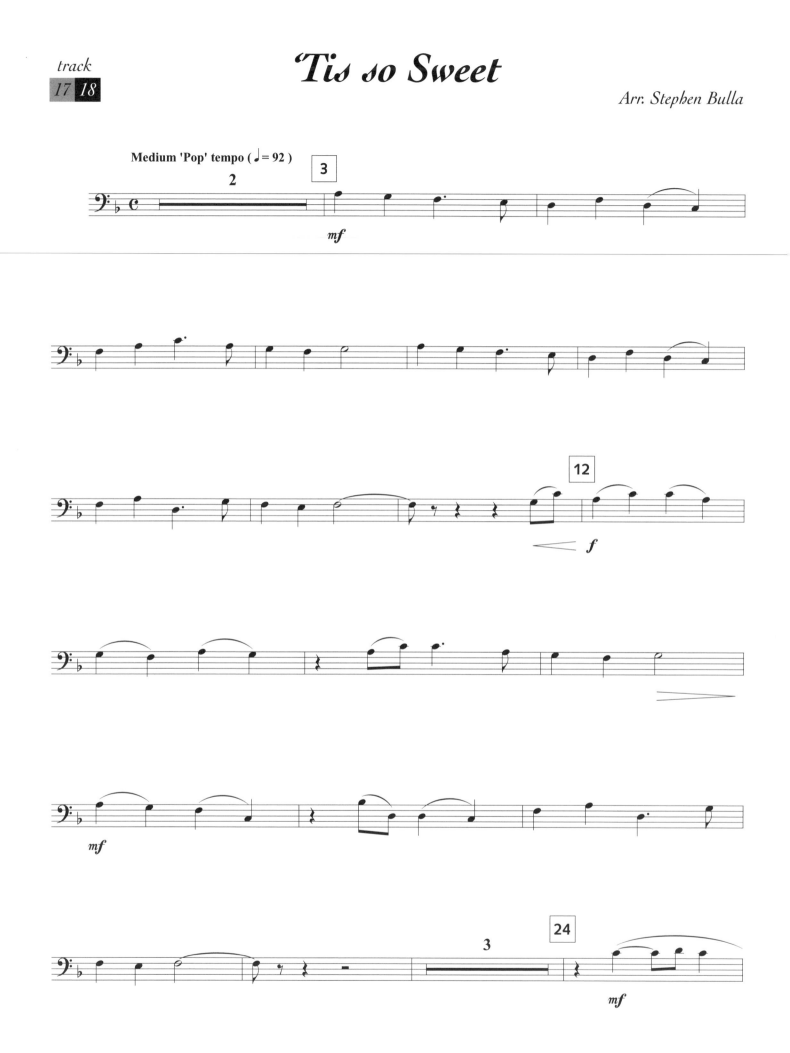

'Tis so Sweet

Sweet Hour of Prayer

Arr. Stephen Bulla

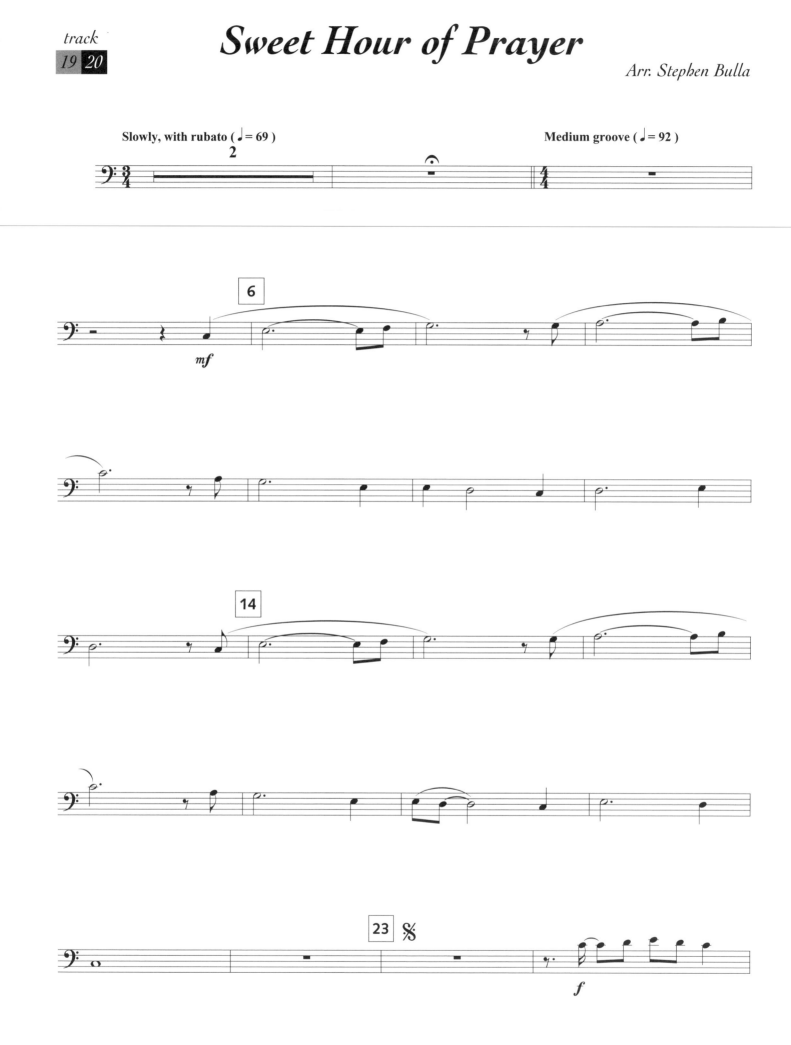

Sweet Hour of Prayer

In the Sweet By-and-By

Arr. Stephen Bulla